The Fairy Godmother's Guide To Dating and Mating

Diane Conway

BookPartners, Inc.
Wilsonville, Oregon

BookPartners, Inc.
P.O. Box 922
Wilsonville, Oregon 97070
503-682-9821

Dedication

To Brian
This time the fairy godmother got the
prince.

Acknowledgements and Thanks

Brian Conway for loving me, always believing in me and making me laugh. Together we make this fairy tale possible.

My Higher Power who made my life and this book possible.

Leila Adams, my grandmother, who prayed from the day I was born for me to get married.

Karen Warner for telling me I'm funny and should do something with it.

Pat Haddock for never letting me forget I want to write.

Annie Lamott who encouraged me, made me laugh and refused to write it for me.

Pamela Van Beekum for taking the rough-rough draft and whipping it into shape.

To all the men who didn't work out — Thank God!

To Ursula and Thorn Bacon of BookPartners. When we met it was like the scene from *ET* when Drew Barrymore sees ET in the closet. "Eeeeeek! The perfect match!" You are the publishing princess and prince I knew would come.

Dated every dysfunctional man in America?

Table of contents

To thine own self be true;
And thus it follows
As day follows night,
You cannot be false to anyone.

Wilhamena Shakespeare

Introduction

Fairy godmothers have traditionally appeared to young girls, but it is grown women who need magic and miracles.

We don't need the guidance now that we required at 17, but we do need a fairy godmother who understands that we've dated every dysfunctional man in North America, and still want to believe that there is a prince out there. We need someone to advise us who has been through the mill, been knocked down, but who has gotten up, dusted herself off, bought the new

Lancome anti-aging moisturizer, a black leather skirt and says, "Hell, I may be down, but I am not out!"

There is a fairy godmother within us all when we come to realize that life is hard, that it hurts, and it certainly is not fair, and we have to live it with some grace (and occasional tizzy fits) anyway. She has her feet on the ground, is reality-based and sees the irony and the humor of it all. Steve Allen says, "Comedy is tragedy plus time." Well, we'll have plenty to laugh about as soon as the pain lets up a little.

∞

This little guidebook I've written shows you that there is humor, even if it is dark. When we are too bruised to laugh it shows us that there is power in our anger. Laughter produces a small window of hope, a new perspective — a new view. It may be as simple as just hearing another woman's pain and thinking, "Oh, my God, me too! I am not alone."

We need a fairy godmother with a few wrinkles and rolls, and some scars, a past, some baggage —

enough to be compassionate. And we need her to have occasional hormonal mood swings, so she can kick our butts when we need it.

All of us have this fairy godmother inside, the wise, loving one, the still small voice that whispers, "You are okay, honey, you are a divine creation, unique and wonderful, and only you can do and be the special things you were put here for." She's kind, even when butt-kicking, and she never tells you to feel guilty. She tells you to love the small spark of your unspoken dream.

Sometimes, she'll be full of wise counsel, and sometimes she'll be a know-it-all friend who barges in and cleans house. Sometimes our stories as women are funny to her and sometimes they are pitiful, just like life. We can learn to love it all and honor ourselves through it all. If we can laugh at it, we can live with it. People love to tell us, "When life shuts one door, it always opens another." I like what a friend said, "Yeah, but the hallways scare the hell out of me!" This little book is your guide for the hallways.

Your fairy godmother is here to tell you that in

spite of your past experience, you can have a good relationship. There is a man out there somewhere for you. At this moment he is feeling the same things you feel; he thinks it will never get any better either. And one day, you will find each other and write a new story. I know, because it happened for me, and if it can happen to me a slightly compulsive woman, a free spirit, riddled with abandonment issues, it can happen for you.

1

Amazing Grace

Once upon a time, when I was 19 years old, I went to Europe. In Brussels, I bought a delicate, hand-made lace wedding veil. I just knew I would need it real soon. I had always wanted a mate. Since about the age of 17, I have been praying for my prince.

It will tell you about my brilliance in picking princes when I say that my first affair started in the janitor's closet at the office Christmas party. He was married and I was drunk.

Eventually, I stopped thinking about the veil. I

packed it up in some blue tissue paper and stored it in the back of whatever closet I was using. A couple of times I almost got married, but they were more of the "let's drive to Vegas tonight" variety. They would have been disasters. To make a long story short, I had many affairs and experiences. I nearly did myself in with booze and drugs. I lived all over the place. I lost myself, my friends and my possessions.

A small spark inside of me still believed in fairy tales, even though it was hard to believe when I felt empty. During that time, I would grasp at any relation-ship, even the most inappropriate, and I would have sex when all I really wanted was closeness.

In 1974 — a turning point — drinking, brought me to the edge of total defeat. I knew such loneliness and despair. I asked for help and met a group of people in recovery who had been through the same things I had. These people loved me when I could not love myself. I discovered I was not a bad person trying to get good, but a sick person trying to get well.

My self-esteem grew, but I continued to have painful relationships with men. Sometimes I would swear off men all together. I thought I was too defective to fix, and certainly too weird to have a marriage.

∞

In 1981, I moved to San Francisco. I was 36 and I felt I had dated every dysfunctional man in North America.

Geraldo was encouraging. He said, "Research shows, a woman over 35 has a greater chance of being taken hostage by a terrorist group than of finding a lasting love or marriage." Oh, thank you for sharing, Geraldo!

After a particularly baffling affair was over, I got down on my knees on my kitchen floor and swore a solemn oath to myself that I would rather be alone the rest of my life than to date another crazymaker.

When I swear oaths it seems like the Universe likes to pass one more by me, just to see if I am serious. I hate it when that happens. Sure enough a man came along and explained that although I was irresistible, monogamy did not appeal to him. I resisted.

I started a vigorous program of cleaning out the ideas and beliefs in myself that were not working for me. I got involved in a women's group and I worked on believing in myself.

Another man came along; he was very cute and very sweet. Brian is six feet tall, with curly brown hair, blue eyes and classic good looks and manners. He had also just moved to San Francisco. We were both interested in finding a better life and working on ourselves.

On the 30th of May, 1994, we celebrated eleven years of the best and only marriage either of us ever had! Geraldo was wrong!

When we first started dating, I discovered he was 12 years younger than I. He was 24 and I was 36 — I find this to be the perfect combination! Age was never and issue with him, so I did not make it a big deal (smart girl, at last).

∞

In hindsight, it all seems to make sense now. Growing up in South Carolina, my mother had me start praying for a mate when I was five years old. I was down on my knees saying, "Now I lay me down to sleep, send a man who is not a creep — or a cousin..."

At the age of 24, I had no prospects on the horizon and I prayed, "Okay, God, I am ready. I am looking good. I have a job. My life is ahead of me. Send him now." At 30, I was getting desperate, "Okay, God, I have learned all my lessons. I would make a better decision now. I am ready, maybe over ready." Then at 35, on the verge of terror and panic, I shook my fist and screamed, "Are you deaf up there? Haven't you heard a word I am saying?"

Now, I believe that all those years the Higher Power was looking down saying, "Be patient Diane, the one I've selected for you is growing up as fast as he can … he is only in the sixth grade!"

When I marched down the aisle at the advanced age of 37 and a half, I did it in snow white from head to toe. I wore a lacy Victorian wedding dress with a flower wreath in my hair, and my Belgian lace veil.

Our friend, Sarah O'Donough played *Amazing Grace* on the organ and everyone sang and cried, especially me. It was magical, spiritual and miraculous. Brian says it was the proudest day of his life.

No one said a word about a really worldly woman with a lots of experience wearing white on her wedding day. My philosophy is, if you lay off relations for awhile, it grows back and you are better than a virgin, you are a born-again virgin.

And remember what the fairy godmother said to Cinderella:

No matter how your heart is
grieving,
If you keep believing,
The dream you dream will come
true.

2

Steps To A Divine Relationship

I believe it is God's will for you to have a loving, caring mate, who is totally in love with you. We did not create the desire and longing for a mate, we were born with it. I believe that we were created with this longing and when we come together with our mate it is a divinely blessed union.

So many women have become discouraged by their attempts to have a good relationship that they have almost given up hope. No matter what your experience, it is possible to have a fulfilling and loving relationship. Remember, all it takes is one. There may be nine million nit-wits out there, but you just need one good man.

He can come into your life even from the other side of the planet. This is true because the Universe and our mind create what we need and deliver it to us. We are not looking around and trying to pick a mate from available choices. (I used to sit in restaurants, churches, etc. and try to pick the least objectionable man, as if the Universe wanted me to go on a steamed spinach diet and be really miserable. Now that I have a cute, loving and adorable man, I laugh at having had that limiting thought.)

For instance, Brian and I moved to San Francisco independently, in the same month, from two different parts of the country. When you are ready, God literally moves mountains.

∞

I realized that my way of attempting to have relationships did not work, whether it was because of my painful past or just bad luck. Realizing this gave me relief, I just sort of gave up and knew I needed a complete change of consciousness. The best thing for me to do was to ask for help in this baffling area and to believe that something more powerful was helping me.

Next, I listed the men I had been involved with and how each had affected me. I saw my patterns, and that those patterns kept me feeling hurt and disappointed. Most of them produced negative feelings about myself. Often I was trying to make a relationship work which was hopeless from the beginning, I was barking up the wrong tree.

∞

When we choose a man who is not emotionally there for us — he is not willing to commit to a relationship — we are spinning our wheels. It takes two willing people to make a relationship. At first a man may not be willing to commit to "till death do us part," but he should be willing to give you an indication that he will be around for a while.

Brian and I were friends for about five months before we became intimate. I was able to see him in different situation; he was a kind and funny person. After we become lovers, I had so many 'hangover' fears from the past, I was afraid nothing would ever work for me and that I would always lose. I had plenty of previous heart breaks to look back on.

I asked my best friend, Mary Beth, "What if it does not work out, what if…? what if...?"

She said the wisest words:

If it is right, there is nothing you can do to mess it up. If it is wrong, there is nothing you can do to fix it. So relax and trust and enjoy.

At some point we must confront the fears that chatter in our heads: "I will never have a good person in my life. All the good men are taken. I always get hurt." We all have these fears and these negative voices. We must learn to talk back to them firmly.

A good way to do this is to write the fears on the left side of a piece of paper and write a positive answer on the right, like this:

Negative Thought	**Positive Answer**
It will never work for me.	Says who?
I am a loser.	No, you are not.
It's not possible at my age.	I will be the first.

Write every negative thought you have and answer each one with a positive reply until the voices stop. Those voices will get tired.

My next step, was to come to believe that I was a loving, desirable woman, and that a man would be lucky to have me in his life. This was a lot of work because I, like most people, had years of conditioning which affirmed that I was not worthy and not good enough. Now, I also know that I am loving and desirable without a man in my life. I am complete with or without a relationship.

I did lots of self-love producing activities: long walks in nature, eating healthy, honoring my body and my mind while enriching it with good music, plays and books. I changed my thinking about myself by catching myself when I put myself down. I did daily affirmations to put strong new ruts in my brain.

Affirmations

I deserve love, I am loving, desirable and in demand.
I am the cutest of the cute. I deserve a man and lots of loot.
It is God's Divine Will for me to have a loving mate.
I accept it now.

The purpose of affirmations is not to convince the Higher Consciousness that I am worthy and wonderful. The great Spirit is trying to get my attention to convince me all the time that I am Its lovely child. The purpose of affirmations is to convince myself.

∞

One day, after months of affirmations, prayers and inner work, I got what I call the "Divine Click." I knew right to the core of my being that now it was God's will for me, Diane, to have a loving partner and life mate now. Brian and I got together a couple of weeks later.

∞

In every endeavor there comes a time when we need to know where we are going. We shouldn't rush, but we should not put off acting out of fear. The most important thing I did for myself was to make a decision that I was not going to compromise on what I wanted. I wanted a committed loving relationship that would lead to marriage. As I said before, I made a vow to the Universe.

When Brian and I had been intimate for a month or so, I sat him down on a park bench in Washington Square Park, in North Beach, and said something like this, "What are your intentions? I'm not getting any younger and I am not willing to waste my time on a relationship that is not going anywhere."

I am pretty sure that this would not be considered good strategy by some *Cosmo* experts, but it worked for me. You see, I was really willing to let go of this relationship if it was just going to be another crazy-making thing for me. He was a little shocked, but he really liked me, and was beginning to love me. That is the key; either they do or they don't.

If you ask for assurance from someone who really cares, it will not scare him off. You do not have to play silly guessing games. I am too old and wise, and love myself too much, to pull daisy petals. I went straight to the source and asked the questions.

He responded, "The way I feel today, I want to be with you for a long, long time.

I could hear the Hallelujah Chorus singing all over Washington Square Park. I could almost bet the bells in St. Peter and Paul's rang.

What freedom and dignity to go out on a limb and say, "This is what I stand for, this is what I want and deserve. I insist on getting what honors me."

I thought back to the months when I had been in that same park with a man who was extremely hand-some and seductive. He had come on like gangbusters — "I have never felt like this about a woman before." But there were definite clues in the beginning that he was not emotionally available and I had ignored the signs because I wanted him so. The pain was so great from this experience that now I can spot a heart break-er a mile away.

There is a story about a man who found a half-dead snake in the road on a freezing winter day. He felt sorry for it, took it home, fed it, made it warm and nursed it. One night while the man slept, the snake crawled into his bed and bit him on the neck, a poisonous bite. The man was shocked and exclaimed, "Why did you bite me? I saved your life." The snake replied, "Because it is my nature to bite, and you knew I was a snake when you picked me up."

I got a merit badge
in snake identification,
And I did not go back to the
Girl Scouts for it.

There may
be fifty
ways to
leave your
lover, but
all you
need is
one.

3

Wash That Man
Right Out of Your Hair

We must release and let go of the men who are
not right for us. Hanging onto a situation that does not
nourish and fulfill us eats away at our spirit and self
esteem. Waiting for "him" to finally come to his sens-
es and realize how wonderful you are could prevent
you from finding the love of your life.

We allow men to get away with bad and incon-
siderate behavior because of our belief in scarcity —
that there are not enough good men. I will have to
admit that it frequently looks like the pickin's are on

the slim side. In truth, there is someone waiting for us, but we have to go out on a limb and let go.

We fall into the trap of telling ourselves, I have to make allowances for him because he:

Is just out of bad relationship.

Had intimacy issues from childhood.

Is busy with his (pick one) new job, car, model airplane.

Is going through a growth period.

The bottom line is that if he is not at your front door on a regular basis, chances are that he is not interested enough. If we like someone, we will *make* time to be together. Usually men who flake out, do not have time and break dates either are trying to have a sexual relationship without the caring and consideration, or they are trying to let you down easy, so they will not feel guilty.

We frequently let men get away with (even make excuses for) behavior that would be unacceptable in a business setting or with a friend.

Here's what happened to my friend, Petunia. She dated a man a few times. He started backing off. He called but did not ask her out. This confused her. He made two dates and broke them both. Petunia is no dummy, but she was uncertain about where she stood.

One of Petunia's friends encouraged her to give him more chances.

I said, "You are giving him more chances to let you down. Forget this one, he is not worth it."

A good way to stop the insanity is to put the situation on paper. See the reality in black and white. Make a chart like the following:

Actual Events	**What I Really Want**
He broke the last date.	He sent me flowers.
He never calls.	He calls daily.
His is busy.	He makes time to see me.

Women are so good at caretaking
that men do not even have to
make their own excuses;
we do it for them.

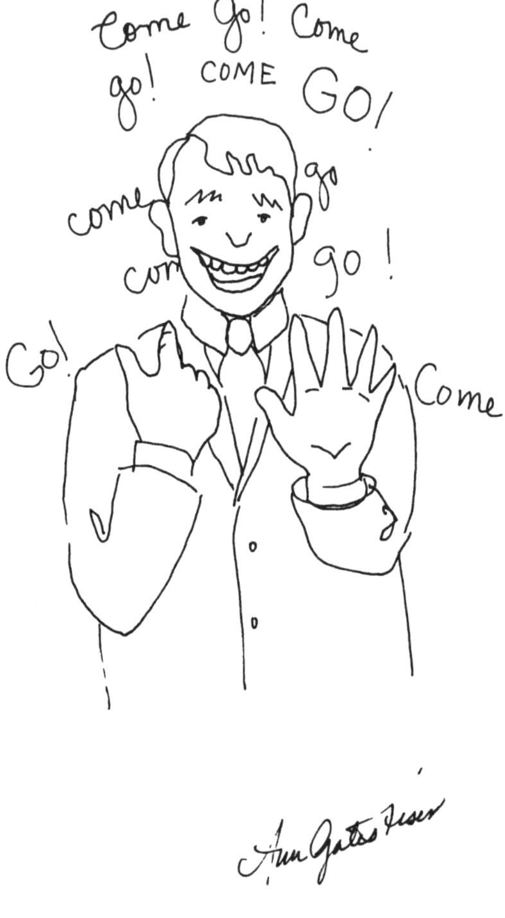
Come Go! Come
go! COME GO!
come
go
com
go !
Go!
Come

Look at your list and ask yourself, "Would I advise a friend to stick with this man or would I advise her that she deserves better?"

Crazymakers play that come-here- go-away game. He will say, "I really like you but .... I could not call because the dog ate my phone book." When in doubt about the whereabouts of a man, chances are he is not in the emergency room moaning your name.

He is probably:

> Out with a new conquest.
>
> Sleeping.
>
> Channel surfing.

Do not call him.

*I could miss the real love of my life
waiting for Mr. Nit Wit,
who has not called in three
weeks.*

The bottom line is … if a person likes and cares about another, he will make every effort to please her, treat her well and most importantly spend lots of time with her.

You know that when you are in love,
you would drive thirty miles
to spend thirty minutes with your love.

This is the way love acts.

I got so sick of having these unfulfilled relationships that I was willing to risk not having any relationship in order to get what I deserved.

I was willing to spend the rest of my life alone with a good book.

In the book, Alcoholics Anonymous, (page 96) there are some lines about working with newcomers. I often paraphrase these to apply to dating:

"Do not be discouraged if your prospect does not respond at once. Search out another prospect and try again. You are sure to find someone wonderful enough to accept with eagerness what you offer." I find it a waste of time to keep chasing a man who cannot or will not work with me. If you leave such a person alone, he may soon become convinced that he cannot live without you. To spend too much time on the wrong man is to deny the right man an opportunity to live and be happy with you.

Do not compromise.

We need to raise our expectations instead of lowering them. The paradox is that what "looks" practical is not true. In recovery programs, we are told to "surrender to win." We surrender our addictions and we get recovery. We need to list what we expect and want in a partner, and really mean it.

And the day came
when the risk to remain the same
was more painful
than the risk it took to change.

4

On Being Real

When I was single, I got so sick of people telling me, "You have to learn to love yourself or no one else will love you." I had been working on loving myself since I was born. I tried to get to the magical point where I loved myself, but I soon discovered that it might take more life times than I had. People don't love themselves all the time and if they did they would be insufferably boring.

Zora Neale Hurston said, "I love myself when I am laughing and then again when I am looking mean." This is what we need to learn; to accept ourselves, however we are feeling. Accept it all. When we accept the so called bad feelings, we can quickly change them. Acceptance is the first step.

Do you know how many first dates you can have in 36 years? Way too many.

I got to the point that when I was going to go out with a new man, I wanted to answer the door in a dirty robe, my hair in curlers and a gooey green mask on my face. I could open the door and say, "Do you want it or not? It may not get any better than this!" Practice not being perfect. So many projects are not begun because if we cannot do it perfectly we will not do it at all.

If you talk to artists, they will tell you that their work does not ever feel completed. They create anyway. I do not mean act your worst and tell the guy every neurosis you have. Be real, be human and do not be afraid to be unique.

Life is a banquet
and most poor suckers are
starving to death.

Roz Russell

Ann Gole Fiser

～

I used to tell a man all my problems on the first date, "I am in therapy for my abandonment issues." That will send him running! A friend of mine gave me some advice. She said, "You tell a man too much, it is none of his business! Tell him some things. Do not say much until you get an engagement ring. After about thirty years of marriage, tell him the rest of the story." I realize that, for years, I had been giving men reasons to reject me. Instead, I began to stack the deck in my favor. What a concept!

Ann Gatewood

5

Loving Yourself

A Special Space

Somewhere in your home create a special space. Find a comfortable chair, maybe a rocker. Set up a small table or shelf and arrange a few things that make you feel good: crystals, candles, stones, shells, fresh flowers, pictures of yourself as a little girl. Go there to pray, meditate, write in your journal and dream.

∞

Personal Journal

Books with beautiful covers and blank pages are sold in most bookstores. Find one you like. Write down your thoughts, troubles, dreams and affirmations. Months later you can look back and see how things have changed. I have the journals that I have kept for the last twelve years.

Write in your journal every night before you go to bed. Get your emotions and thoughts out of your head (where they will drive you nuts) and onto paper. This process is magical. Your willingness to look at these painful feelings takes courage and you'll be rewarded with insights and strengths. Let yourself write anything and everything that comes into your mind. Like, "This hurts so bad. I feel like I'll never get over it. I'm so lonely. Why …? Why …?" Just keep writing.

∞

Visualize

Visualize yourself the way you wish to be and live. Create in your mind your perfect environment. You may learn that you really long to live by the sea and then you can make plans to visit or move there. Create your perfect job, man, vacations, friends, etc. Everything starts with imagination. Albert Einstein said, "Imagination is more powerful than knowledge." Whatever is created on this planet was once an idea in the mind of God or man. You are powerful and you can create your circumstances.

Write down your perfect scenes (maybe in your journal). Do not be afraid to dream. Do not censor or limit yourself.

My perfect day would be ... _____

My perfect home would be ... _____

My perfect job or career would _____

My perfect man would be _____

∞

Use Your Anger

Anger is a spark, it can fuel the fire to change our lives. When we get good and mad we are ready to make changes. The more you let yourself have all your feelings and express them fully, the deeper the healing will be. Make friends with your anger; it is your ally. It will not hurt you, but stuffing and denying it will. Write about your anger (you may find that you have years of unexpressed rage built up). Scream in the car on a country road, pound a pillow, lay on the bed and kick your heels into the mattress. It will pass faster and clearer if you acknowledge it.

Reach Out And Get Friends To Help You

Heartbreak is the time to call in your markers. Let those friends who you've listened to help you; ask them to check on you daily, take you out to lunch, movies and generally divert your attention or listen to you. Tell them: "I just need to talk this thing through, I don't necessarily need advice." Let them babysit you.

If there is one thing women know how to do, it is to get up after they've been knocked down. Yes, we have a Ph.D. in that. We've been getting up after broken hearts, rotten jobs, and bad perms for years. As one woman put it: "Many of the things I've been committed to, I should have been committed for!"

Sometimes our trouble is self inflicted. Other times we walk into someone else's soap opera. We females are survivors.

Survivor Nellie, who knew her powerful attorney husband was having an affair with a female judge, found the phone number of their love nest at the lake and called it. Wouldn't you? He answered and pretended it was not him! Later he said, "You know, I was thinking of giving our marriage another chance, but since that phone call, I know I can never trust you again." Does this take the cake? Can you believe it? Stuff like this happens and it happens to the best of us.

When I met Nellie, she had been brought to my comedy show by some friends; they were pretty much carrying her around, babysitting her, like our friends do when we are certified incompetents due to divorces of various kinds. She was packing up the kids and moving back to Texas. She was hurt, but she was laughing.

When you have to come to the end of all the light you know and are willing to take one more step — either you will be given solid ground to stand on or you will be taught to fly.

Gordan Paul

6

Healing

Things we should have been taught in school: Men and women are different in their approach to love, sex and romance. We don't even call it the same thing. Women call it "making love," men say it's "getting laid." It is basic, biological common sense.

During the dating phase, most men will do or say anything to get you in bed. This is not bad or wrong, it is the way things are. Do yourself a favor and make a commitment not to sleep with a man the first months you are with him. Really get to know him and let the sex be dessert, not the appetizer. When you fill up on bread and butter, you never want the meal.

∞

Carol, 34, met a man and spent a "dreamy" evening with him. He said all the right things. He was considerate, did not rush, was polite, intelligent and well bred. They talked for hours. They told each other their dreams and goals. She told him she wanted a committed relationship and ultimately a husband and a child. He told her he wanted the same things and expressed that in the past he'd made the mistake of getting involved too fast and regretting it.

Carol listened selectively and edited out what she did not want to hear. She thought the feeling between them was so strong and they wanted the same thing. She thought, "We're starting a good relationship." He thought, "Oh no, I've done it again, gotten involved too fast." The next day, he wanted out.

A woman will, at times, say or do anything to get love. When a woman makes love she thinks it means: "He likes me as much as I like him. We're starting a relationship. Call the caterers! I'm getting married in the morning."

If Carol had listened to the cues; "I get involved too fast and regret it," she would have said to herself, "Hey, he just told me what his pattern is and he's trying to do it with me now. I'm outta here! If I want to have a future with him, I've got to take it slow."

∞

Think about it, this is a stranger. Even if you are convinced this is The One, you are putting your trust in someone you don't know.

Health-wise, today with HIV rampant, we aren't only committing our hearts, we may be committing our very lives.

The minute you hit the sheets, you're involved.

The minute he hits the sheets, he's planning to play golf.

This sounds harsh and we don't want to believe it, but these principles are generally true and the sooner we accept them and learn to live with them, the smarter and wiser we will be and the less often we will get hurt.

Remember what Mary Beth said, "If it is right nothing you can do will mess it up. If it is wrong nothing you can do can fix it. So relax."

Everyone gets rejected: the most together people you ever knew — Oscar winners, rock stars, truck drivers and people named Maurice. The only people who never get rejected are the ones who refuse to risk. Not risking is permanent rejection.

When we are faced with the Big R (rejection) we always feel totally alone, alienated, maybe even embarrassed, but definitely like we're the only one. You are not alone. You are in great company. Buy the *Enquirer* or *People* and read about the "heartbreak of the stars." I don't say this to minimize your pain, but to let you know you are not alone, and you're definitely not unlovable just because of this situation.

As Oprah wisely said, "Look at Lady Diana, it looked like she had everything, not just the glass slipper, she almost had the crown." Just goes to show, things aren't always what they seem. We frequently envy things that would make us miserable.

∞∞

Don't blame yourself, and don't abandon yourself. When you try to figure a man out, you are putting yourself in his head. Which means there is no one home in yours. Get back in your head and take care of you.

Put this note all over your house and car:

I will love myself through this and trust the Higher Power to heal my heart.

∞∞

Two years ago, Coreen was having a hard time; nothing was working for her. She confided in me that she was so tired of living that she wanted to end it all. However, she realized that there were a couple of things she wanted to experience to make her life complete. One was to perform stand-up comedy and the other was to play the guitar.

Coreen put together a comedy routine and performed it in one of my shows. She learned to play the guitar.

She got through her dark night of the soul. It took a while; things did not get better right away. We all go through these periods and sometimes people who appear just fine on the surface are suffering underneath. The point is that Coreen's do-or-die list saved her life. By the time she accomplished these two things, her life had changed and she no longer wanted to die. Now she has a job people would kill for. She is paying off old debts and dating a great man.

We all have these deep longings and secret desires to do certain things in our life. Don't depend on a man to fulfill you; take out your list and work towards a goal that will give lasting satisfaction and pride — fulfill yourself first.

One of my do-or-die items was to complete this book. I felt so strongly about it, I stopped and started many times, but it never let me go. I finally printed a few copies for friends, just to get it out in the world.

My do or die list is … _____

∞

Follow your dream...
take one step at a time
and don't settle for less,
just continue to climb.
Amanda Bradley

What Would I Do If I Had No Fear?

My friend, Mary had a lovely home, three wonderfully strange, almost grown children, and was restless and discontent. One Sunday during the NFL play-offs, she walked into the entertainment center of her lovely Southern home and blasted the TV with a shotgun. She scattered the Green Bay Packers all over the den. This was the end of her 20-plus years of marriage.

Healing takes place in strange and mysterious ways. Mary spent from Thanksgiving to Easter, mainly just lying on her sofa in a chenille bath robe. She calls it her Chenille Period. She ate chocolate, read whatever she wanted and grew cobwebs. Then one day, the Chenille Period was over and she got up and went back to school getting a Masters in Goddess Studies.

Because Mary was married for almost all of her adult life, she now likes being single and not having a live-in boyfriend. She does not want to have to "dust around a man." Sometimes we just need "Mr. Right Now" *not* "Mr. Right!"

*I have come to realize
that all my trouble with living
has come from the fear
and smallness within me.*

Angela L. Wozniak

7

Meeting Men

No one can tell you where or how to meet men. But here are a few ideas. First you trust a Higher Power to help and guide you and then:

Walk a dog.

Drive a classic car.

Drive a wreck.

Ask a friend to fix you up.

Go trout fishing.

Do the things you love.

Skydive.

Roller skate.

Go hiking.

Go to Europe.

Carry this book (men are curious about it).

Dye your hair.

Do not dye your hair.

Go to church or temple.

Go to the park.

Go to the movies.

Become a barber.

Become a mechanic.

Become a doctor.

Become a pilot in Alaska.

Do anything in Alaska (it is overflowing with men).

Pray.

Pray more.

Beg.

Know you are cute.

Go sailing.

Take classes.

Go to the library.

Run a personal ad.

Paint your nails.

Paint your toenails (red).

Ride a bike.

Volunteer at soup kitchens.

Take a self-defense class.

Buy tiger print pants and wear them with a *Wonderbra*.

A self-defense class is on my non-negotiable list for you. All women should learn how to resist an attacker and make the world safer for themselves and for others. Being able to defend yourself is empowering. You should have the strength to say "no" in order to have the freedom to say "yes."

∞

When you meet a man, check to see if he has the qualities that interest you. There are things like honesty, loyalty, being single! Definitely you would rule out a man who has been featured on America's Most Wanted. Write down what is important to you:

Qualities I want in a man … _____

Non-negotiable qualities … _____

This list will be valuable when you start telling yourself, "He is really okay," when you know he is not. Look at your list in a non-emotional moment, and realize you knew. You knew you had to have honesty. Be true to yourself. Do not abandon yourself when tempted. You build trust and strength in yourself when you say no to someone who does not empower you.

8

Happily Ever After Stories

Brian and I have been incredibly healing for each other. We have filled the spaces that were empty. Our sense of humor is important. We laugh a lot and do things to amuse each other. We accept each other and we know it is not our job to change or correct the other. I did not have very good role models for marriage, but I do not have to repeat the mistakes I saw. We pray together when times are rough. Neither of us wants children, but we have two dogs, LuLu and Charlie. Our life is so rich and it is a wealth that has nothing to do with money.

∞

Maria, age 53, wanted a mate who was financially stable, liked to travel internationally, and could support her in style. She put a personal ad in the *San Francisco Bay Guardian* stating what she wanted. Letters from men came in and we had a great time reading them over coffee. Some were so funny and many were totally unacceptable. She interviewed men and started dating one particular gent steadily. He had just what she wanted. They are married, and have travelled to Europe and South America, and Maria is free to do her art work.

∞

Cordelia never married and was a virgin at age 80. She met her perfect mate and is happily married.

Nance, age 34, had dated many men but never found the right one. Her secretary met a man at a dinner party, and knew he was right for Nancy. She fixed them up on a blind date and now they are married and content with their two Labrador dogs.

Please write me with your successes, insights and adventures. My next book will include your stories.

Kath's Story

My best friend, Karen was researching stories about the best gifts anyone ever received when this letter arrived:

Dear Karen: It was not until I got home Tuesday

night and I was tucked into bed, when it hit me. The best gift was lying right beside me.

I know this may sound corny but the gift is David, and I got him from God. He was an absolute surprise (almost a shock.) He is unlike any other person I had ever met. He is really a great human being (not to say he has no faults.) I believe we are soul mates, although I do no understand how souls can recognize each other in our present state of being. When I met David at the office, where we both worked, I was dating some guy who you would say was a "Class A" jerk. Dave was my buddy. We played on the company volleyball team together and had long talks everyday. I was not looking for anyone and besides, David was too young. David had other ideas. Soon, I was dumped by this jerk who was so cheap, the only way he would take me to dinner, was if he had two-for-one coupons.

David and I hit it off like best friends from the start. Six months into our friendship, he secretly slipped a three-page letter onto my desk. David, by profession is a writer (and a good one), so his letter said in lengthy detail what he truly thought of me and how he would like to be more than friends. I thought, "Oh, my God, this is weird!" At the same time, I was flattered that he was having feelings like this for me and touched that he was expressing them. I could not believe it — Dave, that super, thoughtful, gentle, funny guy really liked me. What a surprise.

I still find it hard to believe that I have such a gift. At least, it has always felt like a gift, because it was so unexpected and people like him are very, very rare.

Kath

∞

I have one last message for you: I've written this book to provide a little of what the world needs more of — hope, humor, courage and inspiration to keep going. Do not quit before the magic works.

To order additional copies of:

The Fairy Godmother's Guide To Dating and Mating

Please send ___ copies at $11.00 for each book; plus shipping and handling, $3.00 for the first book, $2.00 each additional book in the same order

Enclosed is my check or money order for $_____ or

[ ] Visa   [ ] MasterCard   Exp. ___/___

_____

Signature _____

Name _____

Address _____

City/State/Zip _____

Phone _____
(Advise if recipient and mailing address are different from above.)

Return this order form to:
BookPartners, Inc.
P.O. Box 922, Wilsonville Oregon 97070
503-682-9821

For Credit Card orders
Call Toll Free: 800-895-7323
Fax: 503-682-8684

Diane Conway is available for keynotes and comedy performances for conferences and conventions.

Call or fax:
415-491-4338